GALAXY OF SUPERSTARS

98°	Faith Hill
Ben Affleck	Lauryn Hill
Jennifer Aniston	Jennifer Lopez
Backstreet Boys	Ricky Martin
Brandy	Ewan McGregor
Garth Brooks	Mike Myers
Mariah Carey	'N Sync
Matt Damon	Gwyneth Paltrow
Cameron Diaz	LeAnn Rimes
Leonardo DiCaprio	Adam Sandler
Céline Dion	Will Smith
Sarah Michelle Gellar	Britney Spears
Tom Hanks	Spice Girls
Hanson	Jonathan Taylor Thomas
Jennifer Love Hewitt	Venus Williams

CHELSEA HOUSE PUBLISHERS

GALAXY OF SUPERSTARS

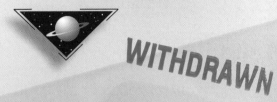

Jennifer Aniston

Mike Bonner

CHELSEA HOUSE PUBLISHERS
Philadelphia

Frontis: Talented and beautiful, Jennifer Aniston is one of Hollywood's most recognized and celebrated stars.

CHELSEA HOUSE PUBLISHERS

Editor in Chief: Sally Cheney
Associate Editor in Chief: Kim Shinners
Production Manager: Pamela Loos
Art Director: Sara Davis

Produced by
21st Century Publishing and Communications, Inc.
New York, New York
http://www.21cpc.com

The Chelsea House World Wide Web address is
http://www.chelseahouse.com

First Printing

1 3 5 7 9 8 6 4 2

Library of Congress Cataloging-in-Publication Data

Bonner, Mike, 1951–
    Jennifer Aniston / Mike Bonner.
        p. cm. — (Galaxy of superstars)
    Includes bibliographical references and index.
    Summary: Describes the life and work of the actress known for her
role in the television show "Friends."
    ISBN 0-7910-6465-4 (alk. paper)
    1. Aniston, Jennifer—Juvenile literature. 2. Actors—United States—
Biography—Juvenile literature. [1. Aniston, Jennifer. 2. Actors and
actresses. 3. Women—Biography.] I. Title. II. Series.

PN2287.A62 B66 2001
791.45'028'092—dc21
[B]   2001042095

CONTENTS

1

CROSSROADS

Spring and summer of 2000 were filled with incredible excitement for Jennifer Aniston. In May, Jennifer and her five costars on the hit television comedy *Friends* got raises that boosted their individual salaries to $750,000 per show over two years. All told, the young actress enjoyed a $20 million payday. Then on July 29, Jennifer appeared at the beginning of a long aisle, wearing a beautiful wedding dress. The bright California sunshine highlighted the floor-length silk and satin bridal gown that clung to Jennifer's figure. She carried a fragrant bouquet of Dutch Vendela roses in her hands.

Jennifer followed gaily-dressed flower girls, who were happily strewing petals and blowing bubbles. One of them was Jennifer's niece, the daughter of her half-brother, John Melick, and his wife, Shannon. Everyone in the wedding party was smiling. This must have been one of the most poignant experiences in her life so far. Today was the day that Jennifer Aniston was marrying the intense, handsome film star Brad Pitt.

More than 200 guests were assembled on either side of the aisle, their faces intent on the bride. It was the biggest celebrity wedding of the year. The only comparable wedding had taken place the year before, when another *Friends* costar,

In 1998, Jennifer Aniston and Brad Pitt went on a first date arranged by their agents. Two years later they would be married in an elaborate ceremony among family and friends.

Courteney Cox, married actor David Arquette.

Even by Hollywood standards, Jennifer and Brad's wedding was a big event.

The media had speculated about a Pitt-Aniston wedding for months. The press coverage grew particularly frenzied after Jennifer flashed a glittering engagement ring at a Sting concert just before Thanksgiving, 1999. Although Jennifer was a wealthy and successful actress, the romantic love she had always craved in her life had been missing.

The couple had selected an elegant venue for their wedding. Perched on a hillside overlooking Malibu, the lush garden setting was heady with the scent of colorful sprays containing 50,000 flowers. Celebrity watchers estimated that the cost for the festivities was in excess of $1 million.

As a six-piece band struck up the classic song, "Love Is the Greatest Thing," Jennifer's father John Aniston, a distinguished-looking man in his sixties, smiled and took his daughter's arm. For 12 years, John Aniston had played the part of Victor Kiriakis on the long-running daytime soap opera, *Days of Our Lives.* Now he filled his role perfectly as father of the bride.

The guests in front caught their first close-up view of Jennifer as she approached the canopied altar. They oohed and aahed over her stunning gown, handmade by Lawrence Steele, a dress designer to the stars. It was cut low in the back and decorated with scads of tiny glass beads.

Besides her beautiful gown, Jennifer's hair was another object of much attention. When Jennifer first appeared on the scene in the mid-1990s as one of the new stars of *Friends,* women across the country immediately started copying her unique hairstyle. Sure to be imitated on this special day, careful attention had been paid to

Friends star Jennifer Aniston and Brad Pitt were married on July 29, 2000 in Malibu, California. It was the biggest celebrity wedding of the year.

her look as her hair flowed below her shoulders in a sun-kissed cascade.

It wasn't all for show. Despite the emphasis on outward appearances, the wedding clearly highlighted Jennifer Aniston's steely self-determination. She had always insisted on being her own person and made many sacrifices to succeed at her profession. Now she was joining hands with the man she loved. Together, they would create the warm and loving family environment they both dreamed about.

Jennifer wanted to show the world there was more to her than mere appearances. She often resented it when people focused on her hair and ignored the effort that went into her acting. She had risen from a modest background to make herself an instantly recognizable star. Like her fabulously successful husband, Jennifer had been lucky, but she had also worked very hard.

No one was more aware than Jennifer that her career accomplishments were close to amazing. At the same time, she was aware that success had occurred only after *Friends* became a hit with television viewers. For the most part, her roles before the sitcom success had not been memorable. Before her success on *Friends*, Jennifer's road to stardom had been far from smooth. In that regard, her show-business story was perhaps a typical one. On the road to fame, people in the acting profession often suffer humiliating rejection. Jennifer Aniston had been no exception. When asked about the price she paid for success, Jennifer answered: "A lot of hurt and rejection."

With the hard knocks behind her, Jennifer's wedding to Brad was not just a personal crossroads, it was a celebration of love. One guest after another remarked about her beaming smile as John Aniston escorted his daughter down the white carpet to her waiting groom.

One person who was absent from the guest list was Jennifer's mother, Nancy Aniston. Tabloid reports said that Nancy Aniston remained at home, "shaking and sobbing," distraught over being excluded from her daughter's wedding.

While not inviting her mother might have seemed cruel from the standpoint of an outsider, it is also sadly true that many successful people become the target of grasping relatives. Some relatives even resort to emotional blackmail to gain favors and gifts. Unpleasant incidents had marred the relationship between mother and daughter in the wake of Jennifer's success.

Nancy and Jennifer Aniston had been estranged for nearly five years, over issues of money and trust. Banning her mother from the wedding was Jennifer's latest shot in their bitter quarrel. Fortunately, the absence of Nancy Aniston did not seem to upset other family members and guests. Nor did it appear to detract from the happiness of the occasion. "Jennifer looked beautiful," her father said afterward. "It was a spectacular wedding."

Everybody who knew the pair said it was the union of a perfect couple. Before going on their first date in the summer of 1998, Jennifer and Brad kept noticing each other at various charity functions. During the previous year, both Jennifer and Brad had ended long-term relationships. Jennifer's romance with actor Tate Donovan fizzled out in April 1998, and Brad split with Oscar-winning actress Gwyneth Paltrow in 1997.

On a date arranged by their agents, Brad and Jennifer discovered they had much in common. Both came from middle-class backgrounds and both shared a strong work ethic. Brad was from Springfield, Missouri. Originally intending to enter design school in Los Angeles, Brad instead found employment as an actor. Between them, the couple felt the pull of a special attraction. Upon getting to know Jennifer, Brad was quickly smitten.

Unlike many male stars in Hollywood, Brad had proven his ability to be content in a long-term relationship. Although his engagement to Gwyneth Paltrow had failed, Brad showed that he was serious about marriage. He was not, as were some of his cohorts, strictly a party guy. Crucial to Brad's appeal to Jennifer was the fact that at age 36, Brad was mature enough to have a realistic view of life. He knew the value of a loving, stable relationship. "She's fantastic, she's complicated, she's wise, she's fair, she has great empathy for others . . . and she's just so cool," Brad said of his fiancée.

Jennifer and Brad wrote their own vows. They promised to love, honor, and cherish one another. Jennifer promised to make Brad's "favorite banana milk shake." Brad promised to "split the difference on the thermostat." A slightly awkward moment—the sort of thing that happens in many weddings—came when Brad's best man, younger brother Doug Pitt, accidentally dropped the ring.

The reception featured a tent with an open side that looked out over the Pacific Ocean. The caterer supplied a huge spread, including lobster, crab, pasta, and peppercorn beef for the guests. The Latin band Gypsy Magic played jazz music while the sun went down in a red-orange blaze. Helicopters hired by press photographers hovered nearby, restricted in advance from entering the airspace above the cliff top. Security precautions were especially tight, since an alleged stalker had been arrested in Brad's home in 1999.

Other than Nancy Aniston, the bride and groom's closest friends and relatives were well represented on the guest list. Almost the entire cast of *Friends* attended the wedding. Cast-comic Matthew Perry was among the hundreds of guests assembling at Malibu High School for the bus ride to the wedding site. David Schwimmer, the actor who played Rachel Green's on-again, off-again love interest Ross Geller, appeared with Israeli actress Mili Avital at his side. Lisa Kudrow, who plays Phoebe Buffay, attended with her husband, French advertising executive Michel Stern. The former model Courteney Cox, known to *Friends* viewers as Ross Geller's compulsive

sister Monica, was there with her new husband, David Arquette. The only missing member of the *Friends* cast was Matt LeBlanc, who was in Eastern Europe filming a movie.

The reception ended with a spectacular fireworks display. The newlyweds then left for their honeymoon. As the guests drifted away in small groups, everyone talked about what a wonderful wedding it had been. "There were big expectations, and this went way beyond that, way beyond," said Jennifer's hair stylist, Chris McMillan. "It was a great and happy day."

Jennifer Aniston seemed determined to have it all. Ambition burned within her. Although her perfect portrayal of the scatterbrained shopaholic Rachel Green might suggest a person who wasn't serious, the love and respect shown for the actress on her wedding day proved there was much more to Jennifer Aniston.

Here is Jennifer pictured with her *Friends* costars David Schwimmer, Lisa Kudrow, and Matthew Perry. The success of *Friends* brought instant fame to the whole cast.

2

THE QUEEN
OF MAKE BELIEVE

Jennifer Aniston is sentimental about babies and loves children. She has said during interviews that she wants to have three children of her own. Jennifer's eyes welled up in tears the first time costar Lisa Kudrow brought her newborn son Julian to the set of *Friends*.

Unfortunately, Jennifer's own childhood was marred by financial hardship and divorce. On February 11, 1969, Jennifer Joanne Aniston was born in Sherman Oaks, California. John and Nancy Aniston brought their newborn daughter home from the hospital two days later. Jennifer was the second child in the family. At home, her half-brother, John Melick, eagerly awaited the arrival of his new sister. Eight-year-old John was Nancy Aniston's son from her first marriage.

Baby Jennifer came home to a modest house in the San Fernando Valley. It was still in the process of being renovated by Jennifer's parents. Despite the clutter generated by the new baby and the home improvements, the family was happy, and Jennifer was a welcome addition.

At the time of her birth, Jennifer's father, John Aniston, was struggling to get his career off the ground. A darkly handsome actor of Greek descent (the original family name

---

Jennifer Aniston grew up in the San Fernando Valley, California. Jennifer's family lived there until they moved to Greece when she six.

was Anistonapoulos), John Aniston resisted being typecast in the typical "gangster" roles. Consequently, he spent much of his time unemployed. While her dad remained at home waiting for a casting call, Jennifer's mother Nancy supported the family with various modeling jobs.

The family faced tough times, and there were occasions when a choice needed to be made between buying groceries or paying the rent. Although the family was well liked and moved easily in Hollywood circles, as a toddler Jennifer mostly wore second-hand baby clothes that were given to her by neighbors. Her brother John scuttled about in worn shoes and patched jeans.

Jennifer was a bright, engaging child. She displayed a vivid fantasy life, and early on developed the habit of inventing imaginary friends. When she was a toddler, Jennifer created a pretend world with groups of tiny invisible playmates that she called the "Little People." One day, her father accidentally stepped on several of them and Jennifer burst into tears. Carefully, John Aniston picked up each of the flattened Little People and did his best to repair the damage. He suggested that Jennifer keep the Little People in the bathtub, where they wouldn't be underfoot. A few weeks passed and Jennifer did not bring up the subject of the damaged Little People again. Her father wondered if maybe they had gone down the drain.

Jennifer also enjoyed pedaling her red tricycle in the backyard. While she was riding around one sunny afternoon, she let out a shriek and began to cry. Her mother rushed outside, fearing that Jennifer had fallen off her tricycle. Instead, Jennifer complained that the grass was "talking" to her.

Jennifer's father, John Aniston, is also an actor and has starred on the popular daytime drama *Days of Our Lives*. When she was young, Jennifer's family often faced tough times as John Aniston struggled to make it as an actor.

Jennifer showed more signs of an intense imagination while she was growing up. Her mother has told the story of seeing her standing atop the coffee table in the living room, getting ready to fly. Though she flapped her arms furiously, Jennifer failed to achieve takeoff. She happily played with her Barbie dolls for hours, putting them through elaborate scenes. Jennifer's brother John later described her as the "queen of make believe."

Although they were eight years apart in age,

Jennifer shared a strong bond with her half-brother. He assumed the role of teacher and mentor to his sister. A Dallas Cowboys football fan, John eagerly taught his younger sister the finer points of team appreciation. Before being allowed into her brother's tree house, Jennifer had to say the secret password, which happened to be the name of a Dallas Cowboys player. Even at only three years old, Jennifer guessed the right answer every time.

During her childhood, Jennifer and her brother enjoyed watching reruns of old television shows. Two of her favorite movies as a young girl were the classic Disney films, *Snow White and the Seven Dwarfs* and the rags-to-riches story *Cinderella.*

Throughout Jennifer's childhood, the Anistons were well known in Hollywood. Another actor of Greek descent, *Kojak* star Telly Savalas, was close to John Aniston. Savalas served as Jennifer's godfather and gave her a pink bicycle when she was old enough to ride one.

Relatives were also an important part of Jennifer's childhood. Her father's mother, nicknamed "Yaya," came to visit whenever she could. The family shared many happy memories of Yaya's superb cooking and warmhearted goodwill. On her mother's side of the family, Jennifer showed a strong physical resemblance to her grandmother, Louise Grieco Dow.

When Jennifer was six years old, her family moved to Greece, where her father had been born. In the Greek capital of Athens, John Aniston hoped to attend medical school. At Nancy Aniston's urging, he had decided to put his acting career on hold.

Jennifer had many interesting adventures in Greece. She visited the island of Crete with her

family. Jennifer toured the ruins of Knossos, renowned as the center of the Minoan civilization in ancient Greece. While in Greece, Jennifer met many of her relatives on her father's side, including cousins her own age. She grew accustomed to the spicy taste of souvlaki, feta cheese, tiropeta, highly seasoned lamb dishes, and tzatziki, a savory yogurt sauce flavored with garlic and cucumbers.

When she was six-years-old, Jennifer's family moved to Greece, where her father had been born. Eventually the family moved back to the United States and settled in New York City.

The longer the family stayed in Greece, however, the more obvious it became that the university would not admit John Aniston. The threat of war hung heavy over the region. Thousands of students from Cyprus were forced to relocate to the University of Athens as a result. When Greek authorities started asking John Aniston to join the military forces, the family decided it was time to leave. After a year of frustration and disappointment, John Aniston's plan to attend medical school fizzled out. The family returned to New York in 1976.

The Anistons settled in a Manhattan apartment. Upon arrival, John Aniston looked up his old theatrical agent. A new role had become available, and the agent said John would be perfect for the part of Edward Aleata on the daytime soap opera *Love of Life.* Jennifer's father auditioned and won the role. At last his career as an actor was on track, and the family, especially Jennifer's mother, rejoiced.

In New York, Jennifer attended the Rudolph Steiner School, a private facility that uses the Waldorf method of teaching. The concept behind the Waldorf method is that each child is a unique individual and that education is an art. At the Steiner School, Jennifer made friends easily and thrived. Intelligent and sociable, she showed an early ability in art and language, the kind of ability that marks a person as unusually creative. Living in New York was exciting too, with all the sights and sounds of the city to experience. New York was also Jennifer's first exposure to a place where the homeless slept on street corners, and muggers make strolling around a bad idea for the newly arrived.

While living in Manhattan, Jennifer attended a performance of the musical *Annie.* She was completely taken with the stage show and told her mother afterward that acting was what she wanted to do when she grew up. An even more influential play confirmed her emerging interest in the theater. Jennifer went with her mother to see the Broadway production of *Children of a Lesser God.* They sat in the second or third row, close to the stage. Watching the actors and actresses perform, close up, strongly affected Jennifer. She was fascinated by the Mark Medloff play concerning the passionate relationship between a deaf woman and a determined male teacher. From that moment on, Jennifer knew what she wanted to do with her life.

Jennifer was nine years old when her parents separated. The divorce came the following year. It hit Jennifer hard. She loved her father deeply, and now he was apart from her. Months would go by when she would not see him. Jennifer complained to her mother that she hated being one of those girls who had to grow up without a father. Maintaining a good relationship with her father grew more difficult as the impact of the divorce sank in. "My dad didn't know how to be a great dad," Jennifer said in 1997. "I was a clown, and always sort of getting into trouble in school, and he thought I was a failure and stupid."

As time went on, Jennifer became less of an outstanding student at the Steiner School. She liked socializing and going out on weekends. Homework was a chore, and her mother had to badger her about getting it done. The Steiner School also required students to learn a musical instrument. Jennifer wasn't interested. She tried the flute but quit after a few lessons.

When something caught her interest though, Jennifer could apply all of her attention to that subject. That finally happened in ninth grade when Jennifer joined the school drama club. One of the requirements for participation in the club was making sure she was up to date with the work in her other subjects. The drama

Jennifer was nine years old when her parents separated and got divorced the following year. The divorce was hard on Jennifer and strained her relationship with her father.

teacher had a strict rule that schoolwork came before club activities. To stay in the club, Jennifer plugged away at her schoolwork. It was a small price to pay for the opportunity to appear on stage.

Near the end of the school year, Jennifer won

the second lead in the class play. Her parents watched proudly as Jennifer put on a winning performance. Afterward, she celebrated with her father at an elegant restaurant.

Before school ended for the summer, Jennifer heard about a special school that promised the kind of training she craved. This was the New York High School of Performing Arts, now known as the LaGuardia High School of Music & Art and Performing Arts. The school is the same one that is the subject of the movie *Fame*. Jennifer had her heart set on attending the school, but getting in took some effort. At first, it did not look promising. But eventually she got an audition, and using a scene from a Neil Simon play, Jennifer passed the audition.

In the fall of 1984, Jennifer enrolled in the New York High School of Performing Arts. At the age of 15, Jennifer's first formal step toward an acting career had arrived.

3

A PROFESSIONAL START

A s with many other things in her life, Jennifer made the most of her opportunities at the performing arts school. Jennifer enrolled the same year that Performing Arts merged with the High School of Music & Art. The 1980 movie musical *Fame* showcased Performing Arts as a hotbed of young talent. In the film, the students at Performing Arts sang, played instruments, and danced on tables. Currently housed in a modern facility in Lincoln Center, the school is simply called LaGuardia by students, faculty, and alumni.

During the years that Jennifer attended LaGuardia, students were offered a rigorous program of training in music, dance, drama, voice, and visual arts. The challenging curriculum exposed students like Jennifer to training designed to make them skilled performers. The program at LaGuardia mixes the arts with a comprehensive college preparation program.

School-age residents of New York City who are able to pass a tough audition are admitted by 10th grade. By the time students graduate from LaGuardia, they are not show-business veterans, but the most talented among them are

---

Jennifer spent her adolescent years in New York City, where her family settled after moving back to the United States from Greece. In the fall of 1984, she passed her entrance audition for the LaGuardia High School of Music & Art and Performing Arts.

able to make the transition to commercial entertainment with ease. Jennifer Aniston is one of LaGuardia's most successful graduates.

While at LaGuardia, Jennifer grew up, changed, and became more independent. She experimented with hair styles, attitudes, and friendships. Sometimes she seemed serious, intellectual, and deeply aware of the world at large. Other times she came across as impulsive and flighty. More than anything else, Jennifer was trying to find herself and see where she fit in.

Jennifer spent a great deal of time alone with her mother during holidays and on birthdays. She felt sad at not having her father at these events. Jennifer bickered with her mother, apologized, and then bickered with her some more. Jennifer's half-brother John had returned to California when Jennifer was 10. Although Nancy Aniston dated and had an active life, she frequently turned to Jennifer as her confidant and emotional sounding board.

In the meantime, Jennifer's talent for comedy was beginning to get noticed. Anthony Abeson, a teacher of acting at LaGuardia, told *Rolling Stone* in March 1996 that he knew in high school that Jennifer would eventually appear on television in a situation comedy. "Even then she had a gift for comedy," Abeson said, "an energy that's not easy to legislate."

Jennifer eagerly took part in the exciting atmosphere at LaGuardia. "Mom, I can't wait to get there because we're improvising scenes and doing unbelievable acting exercises, too," Jennifer told her mother.

At home, Jennifer continued to be troubled by the collapse of her parent's marriage. Jennifer wondered if perhaps she was somehow to blame

for their divorce. Although she was not to blame, the grief she felt caused her to retreat more and more into the world of acting. Jennifer dreamed of a happy life. An inner resolve developed. By going after success, Jennifer was determined to make sure that a similar situation would not happen in her own life. She would be successful, not just as an actress, but also in marriage and family life.

Disciplining herself to study remained a problem. Jennifer was more interested in socializing, acting, and dancing than she was in her studies. At the same time, Jennifer was in a supportive environment where she thrived and was able to display her creative talents.

Jennifer Aniston attended the prestigious LaGuardia High School to study acting. She is one of LaGuardia's most successful graduates.

Both choice and luck had led Jennifer to a place where her natural talent could be refined and challenged. She was also meeting many new people, like Andrea Bendewald, who would be her lifelong friend. During her years at LaGuardia, her friends nicknamed her "JoJen," partly because so many other girls attending Performing Arts were also named Jennifer. She liked wearing all black clothing and favored an oddly cut, crimped hair style. Long bangs completely covered the one half of her face. On the other side, her hair barely came over her ear.

Before going out on wintry days, Jennifer put on a black satin jacket with an embroidered, red Performing Arts logo on the back. Taking the subway or bus from her mother's apartment to school and back, Jennifer drew many looks.

In the late 1980s, it was a popular fashion to wear all-black clothing. The so-called "SoHo" look started on the East Coast and then spread west. Magazines from the time show how this style of dressing dominated fashion. Jennifer's grandmother Yaya didn't know what to make of it. She asked Jennifer how she managed to see out of her right eye and wondered aloud why she insisted on dressing like a widow.

School took up most of her time. Jennifer eagerly rushed to classes in acting, voice, movement, and diction. At LaGuardia, performing arts students like Jennifer had teachers who knew how to guide them toward professional careers in stage, screen, and television production.

A naturally graceful dancer, Jennifer received instruction in both jazz and interpretive dancing. A little bit of her skill in dance can be seen during the musical opening sequence of *Friends.*

Jennifer was growing up and beginning to

express an interest in matters beyond clothing, makeup, and dating. Jennifer's mother tried to lecture her about a modern woman's need for financial independence. Jennifer waved her mother off, saying, "Mom, don't worry. Things will be different with me. What I really need now is to learn how to drive." Intimidating as it may seem, Jennifer learned to drive in Manhattan, practicing in a Honda sedan with a stick shift. She spent hours trying out the gears in a deserted New Jersey mall parking lot until her mother judged her ready for the midtown streets.

Living in New York kept her in touch with her father's family. During vacations, she visited teenage cousins and stayed close to her grandmother Yaya. Jennifer learned to ski in the mountains of upstate New York and looked forward to snow season.

Late in her senior year of high school, Jennifer faced a difficult problem that she had created for herself. Because she had slacked off on her studies, there was a chance she might not graduate with her class. Outside of theater arts, Jennifer was a disinterested, but more than capable, student. The thought of not graduating provided just the motivation she needed to settle down. To everyone's surprise, she suddenly got serious about her studies, and with her mother's help, brought her grades back up.

The burst of academic activity came just in time. A tradition at LaGuardia was the chance to be cast in the senior class play featuring student performers. This annual event is well attended by show business agents and scouts, who are always on the lookout for new talent. The rehearsals were encouraging at first, then discouraging later. Jennifer thought she might be cast in the lead, or possibly in the second lead. As it turned out, however, she was only given a minor part.

She overcame her disappointment and went on with the show. The small part she played was enough to win the notice of agents. The talent scouts saw her acting ability even in a secondary role. After the show, Jennifer had numerous messages to return from agents interested in representing her.

She started looking for stage jobs in New York after she graduated from LaGuardia in 1987. Jennifer spent the next year still living at home with her mother. Her father wanted her to attend college. As an actor, he was experienced in the profession and wanted to spare Jennifer the rejection a performer invariably must go through.

Jennifer appreciated her father's point of view but chose to ignore his advice. She was determined to have an acting career. The relationship between Jennifer and her father was already strained because of all their years apart. John Aniston had left behind a host of broken promises and hurt feelings. He had missed important milestones in her life while he was busy with a new marriage and his second child, a son named Alexander. Jennifer's reconciliation with her father after years apart came in an emotional scene when he admitted his mistakes.

To support herself, Jennifer took a job as a waitress at Jackson Hole, a popular Manhattan burger restaurant. When she wasn't attending stage auditions or hunting for work as an actress, Jennifer served hamburgers, fries, and beverages to customers. The Jackson Hole job was a temporary situation for Jennifer. By then,

Jennifer worked as a waitress at Jackson Hole, a popular Manhattan restaurant, while auditioning for acting jobs. Jennifer had a hard time finding acting jobs until she signed with an agent.

she had decided to devote herself seriously to acting and became very focused. Between shifts at Jackson Hole, Jennifer rushed from one audition to another. She was the girl with the pretty face and the ability to handle comedy. Unfortunately, Jennifer was turned down by one casting director after another. Jobs were scarce for unknowns.

Finding reliable theatrical representation

was also challenging. Theatrical management is crucial to a show business career. Rarely can jobs be found without the services of a good agent. Without decent representation, Jennifer knew there would be little chance of getting ahead. At one point Jennifer used the services of three different agents. Finally, she signed an exclusive contract with the most hardworking of her agents and things started happening.

First, Jennifer landed a spot in the off-Broadway production of *For Dear Life.* Another off-Broadway job came her way in March 1988 when the Orange Thoughts Theater Company produced a one-act Eric Lane comedy, *Dancing on Checkers' Grave.* Jennifer played the part of Lisa, the rich white girl who hangs out in a pet cemetery with her black friend, Dina.

But the best jobs in New York were not coming her way. As was generally the case in her life, Jennifer's looks and talent had gotten her far, but she had dreams of greater success. Jennifer was determined to make the most of her talent and considered moving to California, where the most lucrative acting jobs are cast.

As 1989 began, Jennifer announced to her parents that she wanted to move to California, saying that she felt like she was going nowhere in New York. She needed the opportunities that came from being near the motion picture and television capitol of the world. Her father opposed the move, still wanting her to attend college. Jennifer wanted to get on with her career instead.

Talented and restless, Jennifer showed enough professional sense at the age of 20 to make sure everything was in place for her big move. The agent representing Jennifer in New

York agreed to ask the Los Angeles branch of the agency to handle her business in California.

In her quest to succeed as an actress, she decided to return to the place where she was born. Jennifer left New York in 1989 to live and work in Los Angeles.

4

THE MOVE
TO CALIFORNIA

Jennifer moved to Los Angeles and quickly fell in with the young actors and actresses who bring their dreams of success to the Laurel Canyon area. It seemed as though everybody Jennifer knew was trying to build an acting career. Like Jennifer, they were all unknown, young would-be stars. With no immediate prospects in sight, Jennifer accepted a temporary job as a telemarketer.

Jennifer's half-brother, John Melick, told *Rolling Stone* magazine in 1996 that the move west was a great decision for his sister. "You could tell something was happening, that she was spreading her wings," Melick said.

Few careers set up a person for more hurt and rejection than professional entertainment. Jennifer soon learned the hard way that getting to where she wanted to be as an actress wouldn't be easy. She made a key decision when she decided to shed 30 pounds from her 5' 5" frame. To get the parts she wanted, Jennifer had to conform to the Hollywood ideal. She chose to work on the body shape most sought after by producers. Jennifer spent a full year on her program. She brought her weight down slowly through strict diet and exercise. Taking it off was tough, but Jennifer

---

In 1989, Jennifer made the move from New York to Los Angeles to become a successful actress. She landed her first regular television role in the Fox comedy series *Molloy*.

endured the challenges to achieve her goal.

The combined effects of the weight reduction program and the change of scenery paid off. As Jennifer had predicted, parts existed for her in television programs produced on the West Coast. In late 1989, Jennifer landed her first regular television role in the Fox comedy series *Molloy*. She played the supporting role of Courtney, stepsister to the title character, Molloy Martin.

Molloy was played by future star Mayim Bialik. The show previewed the spunky adolescent role Bialik would perfect in her highly successful 1991-95 television series, *Blossom*. Both of the young actresses were surprised and disappointed when Fox network executives suddenly canceled *Molloy*.

Following the failure of *Molloy*, Jennifer appeared in a 1990 television movie, *Camp Cucamonga*. This light comic turn cast her in the role of Ava, a camper with an attitude.

Another opportunity followed when Jennifer landed a second major series, this time on the NBC network. The new show was called *Ferris Bueller*, a situation comedy based on the 1986 movie featuring Matthew Broderick. The television series featured Charlie Schlatter in the title role of Ferris. Jennifer played Jeannie Bueller, Ferris's bratty sister. The show lasted from August through December 1990. NBC gave *Ferris* the axe just before the new year but waited eight months to air the final episode, called "A Night in the Life," as a summer replacement.

The insecurities of Jennifer's profession started getting to her. Costar Schlatter noticed that Jennifer worried about her hair, which had split ends. "She kept a tiny scissors in the glove compartment of her car," Schlatter said.

"Every so often she'd pull a strand in front of her face and snip it."

Throughout 1991, Jennifer went to auditions and looked for work. Then, taking whatever job came her way, Jennifer appeared in a terrible film, *Leprechaun*. Grisly and badly done, *Leprechaun* is notable in retrospect only for having Jennifer in it.

In 1990, Jennifer landed a major TV role in the new series, *Ferris Bueller*, based on the popular 1986 movie. However, the show only lasted for 13 episodes.

Later, in 1992, another promising show turned up. A new Fox program drew on Jennifer's rapidly advancing comic ability. This was a 1992 variety show called *The Edge.* Fox put the show in a 9:30 P.M. slot on Sunday nights in the fall. Jennifer performed in a host of comic sketches on *The Edge.* The show tried hard to win an audience. The material was sharp and the show was rich in talent. Besides Jennifer, regulars on *The Edge* included Wayne Knight (later Newman on *Seinfeld*), Alan Ruck (from *Spin City*), and Rick Overton.

After *The Edge* was canceled, Jennifer made do with a recurring part on *Herman's Head*, and accepted guest appearances on *Burke's Law*, *Quantum Leap*, and *The Larry Sanders Show*. The shows either failed or gave Jennifer only brief exposure to the public.

Among her friends at the Laurel Canyon house where she lived, Jennifer found many young women who shared her interests and ambition. All of them were seeking work in the entertainment industry. She renewed her acquaintance with her old high school friend Andrea Bendewald and became part of a loose network of young women. The group included filmmaker Kristin Hahn, Collier Strong, and Maxine Lapiduss. Bendewald described the grind Jennifer put herself through before *Friends* caught on: "She spent five years working on shows that weren't great, but she learned how to stay in there."

There were young actors and actresses to connect with everywhere she went. In the evenings Jennifer and her women friends gathered in the woods to form a circle and talk. The group often brought candles to burn and personal items to talk about.

After the cancellation of the 1994 TV series *Muddling Through*, Jennifer got her big break. She was invited to audition for a show called *Friends Like These*.

Another promising role cropped up when Jennifer was cast in the part of Madeline Drego Cooper in the 1994 television series, *Muddling Through*. The plot of *Muddling Through* was standard television fare: After two years in jail, Connie Drego comes home to the roadside motel that her daughter Madeline (played by Jennifer) has kept going in her absence.

It turns out that Madeline recently married Duane Cooper, the dim-witted state trooper who originally arrested Connie. More complications arise because another adolescent daughter, Kerri, lives at the motel as does Sonny, the cheating husband Connie shot. Shooting Sonny was the crime that landed Connie in jail in the first place.

Muddling Through tried to capitalize on the rough blue-collar humor made popular by comedian/actresses Brett Butler and Roseanne. Jennifer did her best to enliven the stale material, but soon it became clear that the half-hour sitcom wasn't going to be successful.

Then she got a break. Right after *Muddling Through* failed, Jennifer's agent brought a new script to her attention. It was the pilot for a show called *Friends Like These*. The original plan called for Jennifer to audition for the part of the compulsively neat Monica. But after reading the script, Jennifer knew she wanted the part of Rachel Green instead.

At first, no one knew if *Friends* was going to be a hit. The show was sandwiched between two popular series, *Mad About You* and *Seinfeld,* but that was no guarantee of success. The main thing *Friends* had going for it was an attractive, talented ensemble cast.

Jennifer was hoping that this show would be a hit. People filming the pilot could tell that the *Friends* crew had great talent. Lisa Kudrow added a wacky element in her vegetarian hippie role. Nothing like her character, Kudrow returned home to Los Angeles from Vassar College with a biology degree in hand. But her brother's friend, comedian Jon Lovitz, persuaded her to try comedy over research.

Lisa studied with one of the best improvisation teachers, Cynthia Szigeti. Her class contained future *Late Night* star Conan O'Brien. After stops with an improvisational troop called The Groundlings and a role in the sitcom *Mad About You*, Lisa got the part of Phoebe Buffay on *Friends.*

Similar serendipitous stories explained the presence of the other cast members as well. Matt LeBlanc did commercials and acted in several failed series before signing on as Joey Tribbiani. Courteney Cox signed with a modeling agency the year after she graduated from high school. Long before taking the role of Monica Geller on *Friends,* Cox won attention by being the girl Bruce Springsteen pulls out of the audience at the end of his *Dancing in the Dark* video.

David Schwimmer had impeccable credentials. A Northwestern University graduate, Schwimmer and a group of his friends put together Chicago's Lookingglass Theater Company, dedicated to creating vibrant works for the American stage. He also played the motorcycle riding boyfriend/husband of actress Olivia D'Abo on *The Wonder Years* before playing the sweet, sensitive Ross Geller.

Of all her costars on *Friends,* Jennifer had known Matthew Perry the longest. They had crossed paths in Los Angeles many times before Perry captured the part of witty, insecure Chandler Bing.

In essence, *Friends* is about a group of six young New Yorkers who share each other's ups and downs with laughter and occasionally, tears. Fans of *Friends* enjoy the uncanny skill with which the writers depict the foibles of young women and men in their late twenties to

Friends was an immediate hit because of the amazing talent of the ensemble cast. All the members of the cast had previous experience in show business and were eager to make their show a hit.

early thirties. Most of the jokes and scenes ring true. The tension behind the episodes has to do with the search each friend conducts for romance.

In one story line, for instance, the character played by David Schwimmer is deeply in love with Jennifer Aniston's Rachel Green. At first she does not take his affection seriously but finally, suddenly, she sees the light. Complications ensue because Ross prematurely gives up on Rachel and makes plans to marry a British woman named Emily. But when Ross gets to the part in the wedding ceremony where he is supposed to say, "I take thee Emily," he slips and instead says, "I take thee Rachel." The wedding ends abruptly.

Jennifer Aniston and *Friends* were an influential success. The casual hairstyle she wore sent countless women to styling salons around the country, demanding copies of the "Rachel Shag." Almost overnight, Jennifer went from Hollywood hopeful to an instantly recognized star. Along with the good, however, Jennifer was beginning to experience a measure of the bad that being a celebrity can bring.

These wonderful times were spoiled by Nancy Aniston's demand for absolute control over Jennifer's finances. The conflict between mother and daughter led to a major rift. What Nancy Aniston wanted from Jennifer was to be her daughter's business manager. Having won success on her own terms, Jennifer was unwilling to surrender control.

FINDING HER WAY

As the audience for *Friends* expanded, Jennifer parlayed the success of the show into motion picture roles. Her film roles ranged from a minor part in the 1996 Edward Burns film *She's the One* to her starring role in the 1999 comedy *Office Space.*

Jennifer also provided voices for two animated films. The first animation was an acclaimed 1998 film, *The Iron Giant,* which was directed by Brad Bird. The second was a Disney cable channel series based on the movie *Hercules.* Jennifer said that her work in *The Iron Giant* was an opportunity that she could not pass by. "I thought it was a very sweet story," Jennifer said. "I wanted to do an animated film and see what that was like. I'll tell you, it ain't easy. It was fun. It's really hard and fun at the same time."

Jennifer received widespread praise for her work on *The Iron Giant.* The film told the story of a boy named Hogarth and his unusual best friend, an enormous clanking robot that streaks to earth in a fireball. The film is based on a story, *The Iron Man,* by British poet Ted Hughes. Set in the Cold War era of the 1950s, critics said Jennifer did a great job as the voice for Hogarth's mother, a hardworking waitress at the local diner. "I love the idea of doing an animated

---

Friends gave Jennifer the confidence she needed to expand her acting. She began to accept offers for movie roles.

movie . . . knowing how much I watched them as a kid. I was so mesmerized and taken into the fantasy," Jennifer said.

In her personal life, Jennifer briefly dated *The Single Guy*'s Jonathan Silverman, *ER*'s Noah Wyle, and Counting Crows lead singer Adam Durwitz. In November of 1995, Jennifer began seeing actor Tate Donovan. He was the voice of Hercules in the original Disney movie.

The success of *Friends* was in full bloom at the time Jennifer met Tate. A mutual friend set them up and something clicked. Within months, they were introducing themselves as a couple, and gave each other romantic gifts. The relationship appeared to be serious.

From 1996 through 1997, the success of *Friends* continued to provide new opportunities for the ambitious actress. Jennifer was swept up in the excitement as much as anyone could be. "For so long I was a waitress, acting on the side," she told *Cosmopolitan* magazine in August 1997. "Now when I drive onto the *Friends* lot, there's a moment of total excitement."

During breaks in the taping of *Friends*, Jennifer managed another small part in another film, *'Til There Was You*. The publicity generated by her television success was hard to ignore. "On the set, we could tell when it was a Jennifer Aniston day because the *Entertainment Tonight* cameras would suddenly appear," *'Til There Was You* director Scott Winant said.

Sadly, not all was fine on the family front. In 1996 Nancy Aniston agreed to tape a segment for the tabloid television show *Hard Copy*. Nancy said later that the producers told her they were interested in doing a segment on the Waldorf method, the teaching style Jennifer had experienced at the Rudolph Steiner school in New York. At one point, the interviewer casually asked a few questions about Jennifer, which Nancy answered at length.

When the interview was shown, the Waldorf method material had been cut and all they played were Nancy's unflattering remarks about her daughter. Nancy's *Hard Copy* interview made Jennifer angry. The breach of trust was not something Jennifer could understand, let alone forgive. Jennifer refused to have any further contact with her mother.

The frosty relationship with her mother contrasted with her improved relationship with her father. Acting on a suggestion from John Aniston, Jennifer made the 1997 film *Picture Perfect* for a $2 million fee. Jennifer played a young woman, Kate Mosley, who craved success in business and love. Kate Mosley was not above comic deceit in her pursuit of either.

The role in *Picture Perfect* put Jennifer in a 100-minute adult comedy film not far removed from her work on *Friends.* It was the sort of relaxed romantic material that lent itself well to her acting ability. The director/cowriter, Glenn Gordon Caron, had already scored with the television series *Moonlighting,* featuring then unknown Bruce Willis and Cybill Shepherd. Like *Moonlighting,* the stars of *Picture Perfect* came through with strong characters and witty dialogue.

Less well received were two 1998 films, *Dream for an Insomniac* and *The Object of My Affection.* An independent film, *Insomniac* had been made before the success of *Friends* and hadn't found a distributor when it was first made. Independent films are mostly speculative low-budget affairs. They fail if no one will exhibit them. On the strength of Jennifer's popularity,

In 1997, while *Friends* was at the peak of its popularity, Jennifer decided to branch out in her acting career. She played the role of Kate Mosley in the movie *Picture Perfect*.

Insomniac was released into theaters. Filmgoers who saw *Insomniac* considered it inferior to *Sleepless in Seattle,* which it copied closely. Better than *Insomniac* was *The Object of My Affection,* a project teaming Jennifer with Paul Rudd, a handsome, soft-spoken actor who had appeared previously in *Clueless.* This film was not a hit either.

On the other hand, 25 million television viewers were tuning in weekly to see *Friends.* On the show, Jennifer's character made the greatest strides, moving from coffee shop waitress to a more glamorous job at Bloomingdale's department store, then to Ralph Lauren's company. Jennifer has the ability to deliver her lines with a naturalness that is hard to fault. Her five costars are also very skilled. Their acting, above all else, carries the show.

Among the viewing public, *Friends* continued to soar in popularity. One factor that boosted the show's success was the impression many had that the stars of *Friends* really were friends. People who work together for long periods of time find the job easier to take when they get along. When they enjoy each other's company, it becomes a pleasure to work together. Most actors at Jennifer's level are professional enough to maintain cordial relations, whether they like each other or not. But the special chemistry that is apparent on *Friends* makes the comedy vastly appealing.

As *Friends* grew more successful with every season, the stars and Jennifer in particular became highly attractive to advertisers. She promoted products such as a L'Oreal shampoo and Windows 95. The Windows 95 ad was a joint effort with costar Matthew Perry. Later, Jennifer and costar Lisa Kudrow were featured in the pages of national magazines wearing milk mustaches, as part of the "Got Milk?" campaign.

Jennifer and Tate Donovan remained close throughout this period. During the summer of 1997, Jennifer took a bike trip with Tate through southern France. Riding a bike 30 to 50 miles per day did wonders for Jennifer, relieving the pressure accumulated from taping *Friends* during the previous fall and winter.

Jennifer and Tate got along well together. She found it easy to date another actor. She appreciated his support, sharing the interests of a common profession. They practiced lines together, and having Tate nearby reduced the nervousness she experienced before going on

One of the reasons *Friends* is so appealing is the chemistry between the stars. The *Friends* cast genuinely enjoys working together.

camera. In her off-hours, it was good to talk to someone who understood the pressures she was under and shared her desire to succeed. In a joking reference to Tate's voice role in *Hercules,* Jennifer told a magazine interviewer that she loved dating a god.

There were also times when they did not get along, however. The idea of having a family of her own occupied Jennifer's thoughts. She was professionally successful, and yet she still felt something missing in her life. One woman that served as a model for Jennifer was her grandmother Yaya. Jennifer said that she admired Yaya for successfully rearing a family after coming to America from Greece. Jennifer was impressed by her grandmother's strength and her ability to prevail in spite of hardship and difficulties.

Coming from a middle-class background, Jennifer developed a fear of becoming too self-centered and isolated by her fame. She particularly disliked the video paparazzi who followed her around, she said, like a silent red eye. After a decade in Hollywood, Jennifer knew how hard it was to connect with people on a personal level once you are famous. She felt the barriers growing between her and Tate.

By 1998 Jennifer's professional success was fully realized. More and more she was appearing in films during breaks in the production of *Friends.* As her success grew, the problems in her relationship with Tate increased. In April 1998 the couple ended their relationship. The split with Tate Donovan hurt, but Jennifer resolved that she wasn't going to let it get her down. She started dating again. At various events she began to notice a man who, reports said, had likewise been hurt by love.

His name was Brad Pitt.

6

CELEBRATION

Jennifer began to inquire and discovered that Brad Pitt was available and that there was no chance that he would revive his romance with Gwyneth Paltrow. She was pleasantly surprised to learn that Brad had also been asking about her. On a date arranged by their agents, Jennifer and Brad felt a mutual attraction.

As soon as they began getting serious about each other, Brad showed his romantic side. While Jennifer was in Texas shooting the movie *Office Space* in 1999, onlookers reported to the press that they had seen the couple holding hands at Austin's Four Seasons Hotel.

On Valentine's Day 1999, Brad rented a jet for a trip to Mexico with their mutual friends. The company of her supportive group of friends helped Jennifer face a milestone in her life—the big 3-0. The guys played touch football on the ivory sands of Acapulco while Jennifer and her friends soaked up the rays while sipping sodas and talking.

Evenings in Acapulco centered around a buffet table that was filled with platters of oysters, shrimp, tropical fruit, and salads. The attention of one of the most romantic male movie stars in America soothed any jitters Jennifer might have felt about leaving her twenties behind.

With the success of *Friends*, Jennifer was at the height of her popularity. The "Rachel Shag" influenced women all over the country to style their hair like her.

The couple took several other trips together as well—to Spain and Portugal, and to high atop the Sierra Nevada Mountains. A crucial journey came when Jennifer went to Springfield, Missouri, to meet Brad's family, including his mother Jane and his grandmother, the 88-year-old Clara Hillhouse.

On her side, Jennifer's father and stepmother had good things to say about the match. "They're a lovely couple, and they're very happy together," John Aniston said.

The indication that wedding bells were in the air came during a Sting concert in November 1999. Jennifer and Brad were asked to come onstage by Sting. When the band broke into a song about diamond rings, Brad raised Jennifer's hand for the crowd to see a large diamond ring glittering in the stage lights. Afterward, Jennifer and Brad played it for a joke, but acted like two people with a secret.

News that Jennifer and Brad were likely to marry would eventually reach Gwyneth Paltrow, the Oscar-winning star of *Shakespeare in Love.* At one time, she told the magazine *Vanity Fair* that losing Brad Pitt had altered her outlook on life. "When we split up, something changed permanently in me," she said. "My heart sort of broke that day, and it will never be the same."

While Jennifer and Brad were dating, the immense popularity of *Friends* kept viewers tuning in weekly. A creation of writers Marta Kauffman, David Crane, and Kevin S. Bright, the *Friends* characters portray young adults at the prime age for marriage in America.

The format helps give *Friends* the tension comedy needs to be effective. Since its debut in 1994, *Friends* has received 19 Emmy nominations. The Emmy is television's highest award.

The show itself has been nominated four separate times—in 1995, 1996, 1999, and 2000, with the rest of the nominations received for individual performances, casting, and script writing. The show won the People's Choice Award in 2000 for Favorite Television Comedy Series, and the 2000 Screen Actor's Guild Award for Outstanding Performance by an Ensemble in a Comedy Series. Numerous other awards for individual performances have gone to cast members, with Jennifer and Lisa Kudrow sharing the 2000 Emmy nomination for Outstanding Supporting Actress in a Comedy Series.

Although critics agree that the acting and the scripts are top notch, they occasionally dislike the focus on material things that seems to drive Chandler, Rachel, Ross, Monica, Joey, and

Friends has received 19 Emmy nominations since its debut in 1994. The show attracts audiences around the world with excellent acting and writing.

Phoebe. They also wonder if the friends aren't getting a bit old to be hanging out at each other's apartments. This may not be the case. For years, in the time slot following *Friends,* the *Seinfeld* cast explored the lives of a group of even older New Yorkers who dealt with similar situations.

Contract negotiations for renewal of *Friends* began in earnest during the spring of 2000. Lisa Kudrow and David Schwimmer wanted the series to end. They had other lucrative projects in the works. The rest of the cast, including Jennifer, wanted the series to continue. One thing everybody wanted for sure was more money. The cast members demanded a higher salary per episode in addition to more money in syndication fees, the sums performers collect when reruns are shown.

The network, the lawyers, the agents, and Warner Brothers went back and forth until a deal was finally made in May. The salary increase came to $20 million per cast member to be spread over two years. The syndication fee boost was estimated to add another $20 million to each cast member's payment. With *Friends* renewed for another two seasons, Jennifer's financial and professional life appeared more secure than ever.

As she entered her thirties, Jennifer began to take stock of herself and the industry in which she worked. She told interviewers that she was unhappy with the images Hollywood portrayed of women. In an August 1999 segment of *Entertainment Tonight,* Jennifer told interviewer Jann Carl that the tiny-waisted women shown in *The Iron Giant* bothered her. "I mean, how realistic is that? We're already plastering unrealistic images all over the world. Why make it worse?"

Jennifer is part of a growing movement among women concerned about Hollywood's obsession with thinness. In a poll of college health officials,

70 percent said that eating disorders were common on their campuses. The idolization of slender models and ultra-thin celebrities aggravates the problem. "I can tell a girl that what matters is what's going on in her head and heart," sociologist Traci Mann told *People* magazine. "But when she turns on the TV, she sees that what matters is how you look."

Remembering her life before success, Jennifer admits to being nostalgic about her years as an unknown. "You always miss parts of your past," she said to *Rolling Stone* writer Rich Cohen in the January 1996 issue of the magazine. "Back then it was familiar and safe, and now you have no idea what's around the corner."

After marrying the man of her dreams in Malibu, Jennifer Aniston quietly celebrated her new married state. When they are not busy working, Jennifer and Brad are like many young married couples. They like to barbecue at home and watch television. A favorite program is HBO's *The Sopranos*. When they get a chance, they take hikes together.

Observers of the pair seem to agree that Jennifer is a great match for Brad. Pitt's non-Hollywood origins are not much different than Jennifer's own modest background. Though he may have been in show business, Jennifer's father spent long periods of time unemployed during Jennifer's childhood. Also, her years living with Nancy had not been easy, although Jennifer confessed that she had been a difficult teenager.

As Jennifer's relationship with her father improved, her relationship with her mother continued to sour. Since the *Hard Copy* interview, Jennifer had sought to keep her mother out of her life. Sometimes it seemed as though Nancy Aniston was determined to capitalize on her

Here are Jennifer and Brad attending the 1999 Emmy awards together. Like most newly married couples, they enjoy spending quiet time together at home.

daughter's fame, by whatever means. In 1999 Nancy Aniston published a memoir entitled *From Mother and Daughter to Friends.* Nancy Aniston's book sheds some light on what it takes to achieve success in Hollywood, but it is not a book likely to endear mother to daughter. Jennifer has refused to comment.

In October 2000, Jennifer showed up at the California Department of Motor Vehicles to have her driver's license reflect her new married name. Although she would keep "Aniston" as her professional surname, from now on her driver's license would read Jennifer Joanne Pitt. Jennifer rides around in a Land Rover. Having learned to drive in Manhattan, she takes to the California roads with big-city abandon.

Her favorite snack food is chips and salsa, occasionally chips and guacamole. She still likes to draw and paint whenever she gets the chance and treasures her dog Katchina, a shepherd mix. One thing she frankly admits is that she is good at applying makeup. The secret, Jennifer says, is to wear it without looking like you are wearing it. Anything more than a light layer is overdoing it. Jennifer loves clothes, but prefers to remain casual. "I like a pair of comfy pants, flip-flops and a T-shirt." she says.

Close friend Collier Strong said that Jennifer's confidence level has gotten better over the years. "She's come to realize what she needs in her life and what really doesn't serve her anymore." Her hard-won self-assurance has led her to develop a website with friend Maxine Lapiduss. Jennifer plans to participate in chat sessions with teenage girls. The focus will be creative and political, encouraging girls to examine their own lives.

The popularity of *Friends* is such that viewers are familiar with the individual personalities of the characters. When readers reported their character preferences to *YM* magazine in the January 2001 issue, 79 percent picked Rachel as the one they would like to be with when they were looking for guys. Rachel also came in first with 80 percent of the respondents wanting to look like her in a style makeover.

Despite her expertly acted television image, Jennifer is more a conservative homebody than the character she plays on *Friends*. Jennifer's hard-won success came with a price, but the things that come first in her life are things that money can't buy.

CHRONOLOGY

1969   Jennifer Joanne Aniston born February 11 in Sherman Oaks, California.

1975   Family moves to Greece, but returns in 1976.

1978   John and Nancy Aniston separate; they divorce a year later, and Jennifer remains in her mother's custody.

1983   Jennifer joins the drama club at the Rudolph Steiner School.

1984   Takes first acting lessons; enrolls at Performing Arts High School (LaGuardia) in New York.

1987   Graduates from LaGuardia and works as a waitress while seeking New York stage work.

1988   Wins off-Broadway roles in *For Dear Life* and *Dancing On Checkers' Grave.*

1989   Moves to Los Angeles.

1990   Appears in first TV series role as Courtney in *Molloy;* appears as Ava in a made for television movie, *Camp Cucamonga;* lands role of Jeannie in television series *Ferris Bueller.*

1992   Acts in her first film, the low-budget horror movie *Leprechaun.* Wins part on comedy variety show *The Edge.*

1994   Lands role of Rachel Green in *Friends.*

1995   Becomes romantically involved with Tate Donovan.

1997   Has first starring film role in *Picture Perfect.*

1998   Breaks up with Tate Donovan in April; begins dating Brad Pitt in June.

1999   Provides voice for Hogarth's mother in *The Iron Giant;* has starring role in *Office Space.*

2000   Signs $20 million *Friends* contract; marries actor Brad Pitt.

ACCOMPLISHMENTS

Television

1990   *Molloy*
        Ferris Bueller
        Camp Cucamonga (television movie)

1992   *The Edge*

1994   *Muddling Through*
        Friends

Stage

1988   *Dancing on Checkers' Grave*

1989   *For Dear Life*

Films

1993   *Leprechaun*

1996   *She's the One*

1997   *'Til There Was You*
        Picture Perfect

1998   *The Object of My Affection*
        Dream for an Insomniac

1999   *Office Space*
        The Iron Giant (voice of Anne Hughes)

2000   *Rock Star*

FURTHER READING

Aniston, Nancy. *From Mother and Daughter to Friends*. Amherst, NY: Prometheus Books, 1999.

Burlingame, Jon. *TV's Biggest Hits: The Story of Television Themes from Dragnet to Friends*. Indianapolis, IN: MacMillian USA, 2000.

Evans, Andy et al. *Fame: The Psychology of Stardom*. Berkeley, CA: Frog, Ltd., 1999.

Lane, Eric, ed. *Telling Tales: New One Act Plays*. New York: Penguin USA, 2000.

Wild, David. *Friends*. New York: Doubleday, 1995.

ABOUT THE AUTHOR

MIKE BONNER has written extensively about sports figures, collectibles, celebrities, and public affairs for middle school readers. In late 1999, his *Collecting Basketball Cards, a Complete Guide with Prices* was published. During 2000, Chelsea House published three titles by Bonner, *How to Become an Elected Official, How a Bill Is Passed*, and *The Composite Guide to Strongman Competition*. His work appears regularly in *Sports Collectors Digest* and *Sports Cards Gazette*. An avid film buff, he lives in Eugene, Oregon, with his wife Carol and teenage daughter Karen.

INDEX

Photo Credits: